Gardening fun

Pop was visiting us and he had a plastic container.

2

Nat said, "What is in the box, Pop?"

"It is spring and I have been scattering seeds in my garden," said Pop.

"I have some seeds
left for you kids."

Pop lifted up the lid of the full container and groaned, "Oh dear! All the seeds are mixed up!

They have all spilled out
of the packets."

Pop had a go at sorting out the seeds.

"I think this is the pumpkin. This is the sunflower. This is the radish and this is the beetroot."

Pop helped us scatter the seeds in the garden bed.

"Now keep the soil
moist and let the sun
do the rest," he said.

We did as Pop said and soon little seedlings popped out of the soil. Some seedlings were green and some were red and green.

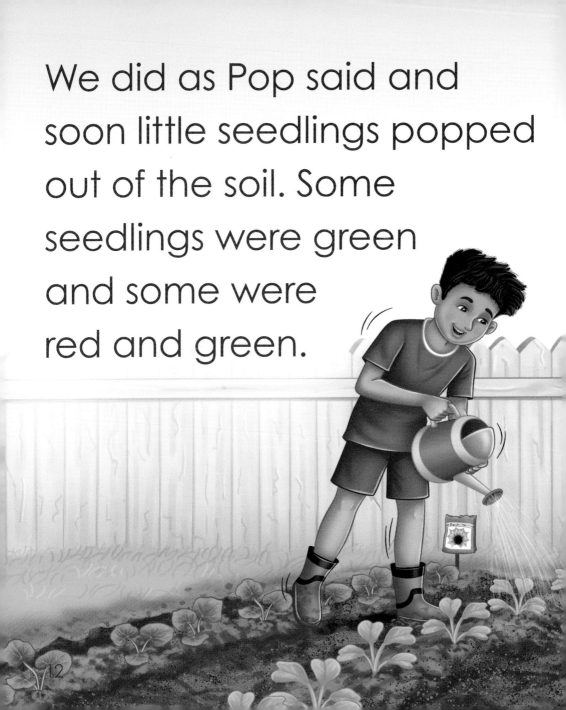

The seedlings started creeping up out of the soil. They got bigger and bigger. Then it was a short wait until we picked them.

Pop was keen to see them.
Sam said, "Here are our
beetroots and pumpkins, Pop."

Dan said, "Here are our radishes."
Nat said,
"And here are our sunflowers!"

15

Pop grinned from ear to ear.
"I love your mixed-up garden!"

Words to blend

plastic	spring	scatter
left	lifted	spilled
pumpkin	rest	grinned
groaned	mixed	sorting
radish	beetroot	packet
containers	helped	soon
wait	popped	visiting

Before reading

Synopsis: Pop gives the children some seeds for them to plant in the garden. The seeds are all mixed up, so what will they find when the plants have grown?

Review graphemes/phonemes: ai oa ow er oi ar ee

Story discussion: Look at the cover and read the title together. Ask: *Who do you think is going to have gardening fun in this story? Have you ever helped with gardening? What did you do? Did you enjoy it?*

Link to prior learning: Display a word with adjacent consonants from the story, e.g. *moist*. Ask children to put a dot under the single-letter graphemes (*m, s, t*) and a line under the digraph (*oi*). Model, if necessary, how to sound out and blend the sounds together to read the word. Repeat with another word from the story, e.g. *started*, and encourage children to sound out and blend the word independently.

Vocabulary check: moist – damp, slightly wet

Decoding practice: Display the following words: *spring, left, spilled, pumpkin, creeping, groaned, sunflower*. See how quickly children can read the words. Encourage them to read without overtly sounding out and blending if possible, but remind them to sound out and blend if they get stuck.

Tricky word practice: Display the word *what* and ask children to point out the tricky parts of the word (*wh*, which makes the /w/ sound, and *a*, which makes the /o/ sound). Practise writing and reading this word.

After reading

Apply learning: Ask: *What did you think of the children's mixed-up garden? Did you expect this to happen, or did it surprise you?*

Comprehension

- Who did the seeds belong to?

- What plants grew from the seeds?

- Why did Pop say it was a mixed-up garden?

Fluency

- Pick a page that most of the group read quite easily. Ask them to reread it with pace and expression. Model how to do this if necessary.

- Ask children to read Pop's words on pages 6–7, making them sound as natural as possible.

- Practise reading the words on page 17.

Tricky words review

our	love	what
was	he	said
full	have	some
you	are	out
my	go	oh